THE JURMALA RUCKSACK

THE AHLBECK BUCKET BAG

THE SIBBY TASSEL

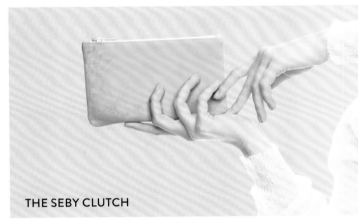

THE SEBY CLUTCH

THE REWAL DRAWSTRING BACKPACK

THE SIERKSDORF WEEKENDER

THE ELDENA 1C TOTE

# INTRODUCTION

When I was living in New York, I would walk up and down Fifth Avenue on a quest for my new favorite bag. But somehow, I could never find the right one. My disappointment gave way to a question: "Could I make my own bags?" I could already sew, and, as an architect, making patterns wouldn't be too hard—at least that's what I thought. Full of anticipation, I enrolled in an accessories design program. My first attempts didn't result in total success, of course, but as the saying goes, "Practice makes perfect!" Finishing my first successful bag made up for all those hours of experimentation. With this book, I want to share some of my favorite bags—designed by me—and walk you through the process of making them. Much of the information in the book is there to help you avoid some of the mistakes that I made during my first attempts.

Leather is a wonderful material. It's durable, long-lasting, and ideal for making handbags and other accessories. If you'd like to try your hand at sewing with a new material and enhance your wardrobe with handmade leather bags, this is the book for you. It will teach you the basics of working with leather and help you get started right away on some simple leatherworking projects. This book includes more advanced patterns as well, so you can create your own personalized handbags, step by step.

In this book, you will also learn about sewing machine requirements and become acquainted with some handy sewing machine accessories, tools, and other items. I describe the characteristics and different types of leather as well as give you tips on buying and caring for it. The hands-on portion of the book deals with cutting the leather and making the projects using leather, faux leather, and heavy fabrics.

Leather is a natural product, and it's worth paying a little more for good quality. When buying leather, look for tanning processes that are eco-friendly and conserve water, and make sure that the animals were treated humanely. The best candidates will probably be leathers from European producers. Many of the projects in this book are designed for a combination of leather or faux leather and a heavyweight fabric. This way, you can work with leather without breaking the bank.

Sewing with leather takes practice. But with the instructions in this book and a little patience, your project will undoubtedly be a crowning success. It's a pretty fantastic feeling to hold your favorite bag in your hands, especially when it's one that you made yourself!

I hope you like the designs in this book and that you find joy in working with leather.

Have fun!

# MATERIALS, TOOLS, AND ACCESSORIES

## SEWING MACHINE

A good sewing machine is indispensable for making leather handbags. Home sewing machines can sew leather if they meet certain requirements and have the right accessories.

Before you begin sewing, it's important to always test all your machine's settings and accessories on a scrap of leather. You should use a piece that matches the leather you will use for your final projects. You can, of course, always rip out the stitches in your leather if you're not satisfied with your machine's settings—but the holes from the needle will always be visible. That's why it's better to test everything twice beforehand than to have to throw away your leather later.

Be aware that computerized sewing machines may switch to default settings when turned on and off. This is another good reason to cut your leather and other materials first, and then, just before you start sewing, test your settings with a scrap piece of leather.

### TIPS FOR CHOOSING A SEWING MACHINE

Some important factors to consider when choosing your sewing machine are the power of the motor, feed mechanism, and needle plate and feed dogs. A motor output of at least 70 watts is a good baseline for home sewing machines. Good brand name sewing machines with mid-range prices are always recommended. These machines usually cost a little more than simpler models, but the investment is worth it. Sewing on a good machine is easier and less complicated—and therefore more fun. Brand name machines also allow you to work more efficiently. You can spend more time sewing and less time adjusting and fixing your work.

It's also important that the parts of your sewing machine run smoothly. When you are ready to buy a new sewing machine, consult a specialized dealer and test out the different models. You can bring a piece of leather into the store and make a sample on the different machines. Don't base your decision on wattage alone. Some cheaper sewing machines have high wattages, but they don't handle leather well at all.

It's a big advantage—essential even—to be able to shift the needle position on the sewing machine to the left and right. This makes sewing zippers and piping much easier and creates a cleaner finish. In addition, an upper feeding system helps move thick fabrics such as leather through the sewing machine securely. Because the material is fed with even pressure from the top and bottom, it doesn't pucker during sewing.

It also doesn't hurt if your machine allows you to switch out the presser foot quickly. However, a wide selection of stitches is not necessary because leather is almost always sewn using a straight stitch.

### NEEDLES

Sewing machine needles made especially for leather are wedge-shaped and available in various types and sizes. Be sure to always test how your particular needle handles your selected leather with a scrap before you start working with your cut pieces of leather. A needle with a smaller number is intended for finer threads and will make a smaller hole in the fabric.

Lightweight and fine leathers, such as goatskin, should be sewn using a leather needle, size 70/10 to 90/14, and a stitch length of 9–12 stitches per inch (2–3 mm). For medium-weight leather, such as faux snakeskin, real snakeskin, or suede, use a size 90/14 needle and a stitch length of 7–10 stitches per inch (2.5–3.5 mm). Heavier weight leather, such as napa, faux upholstery leather, and some suedes, can be sewn with size 90/14 to 100/16 leather needles and a stitch length of 6–8 stitches per inch (3–4 mm). Very heavy leathers require special industrial machines and unfortunately cannot be sewn on home sewing machines.

## PRESSER FEET

The right presser foot makes a tremendous difference when sewing leather. The most useful types of special presser feet are described below.

### Nonstick Presser Foot

A nonstick foot is the primary foot used to work with leather and is suitable for materials that are difficult to feed, such as leather, vinyl, or other alternative materials. It is coated with a nonstick material so the sewn material glides evenly beneath the foot.

### Walking Foot

As an alternative to the nonstick presser foot, you can use a walking or roller foot. This type of foot guarantees that the material is fed through the sewing machine with even pressure from the top and bottom.

### Edge-Stitch Foot

An edge-stitch foot is used to sew a specific distance from an edge or seam line. A common length for this distance is ⅛ inch (3 mm). The edge-stitch foot makes it easier to maintain this precise distance from the edge of the fabric. This makes nice, clean stitches along the edges of the leather.

### Zipper Foot

A zipper foot is used to sew zippers. It allows you to sew close to the zipper without the pull or teeth getting in the way. It can also be used to sew piping. For more information on making and sewing piping, see page 38.

## TIP

If you don't want to buy any special presser feet, there are still a few methods you can use to make it a little easier to work with leather on your machine. See the note about other helpful tools on page 24.

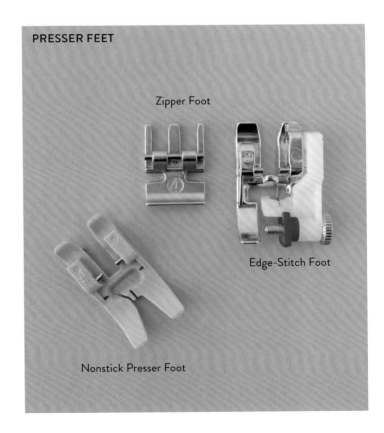

**PRESSER FEET**

Zipper Foot

Edge-Stitch Foot

Nonstick Presser Foot

## STITCH TYPE AND LENGTH

A straight stitch is almost always used for leather. The stitch length should be 6–12 stitches per inch (2–4 mm), depending on the type of leather and how you want the stitch to look. It's important to make sure that the stitch length is not too short. Short stitches poke too many holes in the leather, which makes it unstable and could cause it to tear. For some of the designs in this book, a simple zigzag stitch is also used to finish the ends of polyester and cotton straps.

## THREAD TENSION

Proper thread tension ensures that the stitches on both sides of your fabric look neat and even. For an attractive and sturdy stitch, the top thread should not be visible on the wrong side of the material, and the bottom thread should not be visible on the right side of the material. Thread tension has to be adjusted individually on every sewing machine. Refer to the user manual for your sewing machine to determine the correct settings. To balance thread tension, you usually only adjust the upper thread tension. The lower thread tension should only be adjusted if absolutely necessary.

## INDUSTRIAL SEWING MACHINES

Industrially manufactured leather accessories are often sewn on special sewing machines that are tough enough to handle leather safely and have additional features that simplify the leatherworking process. These include flatbed machines as well as free-arm or post-bed sewing machines, which can also sew smaller accessories using heavy fabrics. If this book makes you hungry for more leatherwork, you might consider purchasing an industrial machine. Used machines are relatively affordable and practically indestructible. Sewing even several layers of leather becomes a much easier task. Any of the designs in this book could also be sewn on industrial sewing machines.

## THREAD

There are various types and weights of thread that are recommended for use with leather. Silk and polyester threads in slightly heavier weights (#30, #40, or #80) are ideal. These types are somewhat thicker and therefore sturdier than normal all-purpose thread (#100 or #120). The higher the number, the finer the thread. Because leather bags and accessories require a sturdy and robust thread, #80 thread is particularly well suited to the task and will produce good results on home sewing machines. Unfortunately, #80 thread isn't as easy to come by these days as finer threads, and the color selection can leave something to be desired. While they can be too thick for some home sewing machines, #30 and #40 threads also work well with leather and are widely available in specialized shops. When sewing leather, always secure the beginning and end of your seams. For visible or topstitched seams, use a single backstitch at the beginning and end of the stitching.

Commercial bags produced on industrial machines are often sewn with #40 bonded nylon thread. The advantage of bonded nylon is its strength. The thread ends can also be knotted easily and then melted together with high heat. Sadly, home sewing machines are seldom equipped to work with bonded nylon.

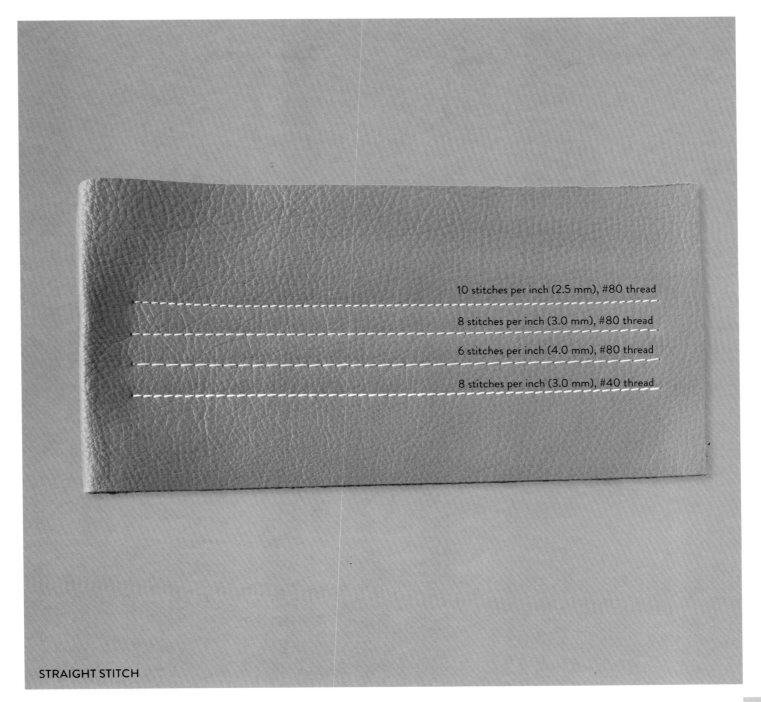

10 stitches per inch (2.5 mm), #80 thread

8 stitches per inch (3.0 mm), #80 thread

6 stitches per inch (4.0 mm), #80 thread

8 stitches per inch (3.0 mm), #40 thread

**STRAIGHT STITCH**

# INTRODUCTION TO LEATHER

There are a few basic guidelines to follow when working with leather. When choosing leather, pay attention to its quality, origin, strength, weight or thickness, and elasticity, and make sure it can be sewn on a home sewing machine.

Leather is not priced by the yard. It is typically sold by the whole hide or half hide (also called a side). Hides vary in size and are measured in either square feet or square meters. Cowhides are relatively large—a half hide of napa cowhide can be 27–38 square feet (2.5–3.5 m²). The edges of the hides can be irregular, and certain parts of the hide have different characteristics than others. The leather that comes from the area along the animal's backbone is the most durable and has a uniform appearance with a fine grain. As you move towards the legs and flanks, the leather becomes looser and more elastic, and the grain becomes larger. For this reason, you want to choose pieces from the middle of the hide the visible parts of a bag, while pieces from the sides of the hide should be used for the less visible parts. In addition to unevenness on the edges, a hide may have holes and small blemishes like insect bites or scars. However, these do not usually indicate that the leather is poor quality. You can always cut around these natural markings.

If you plan to make only a small accessory from a specific type of leather, you can often use remnants or scraps left over from a larger project. Because every hide is unique, it's not always possible to reorder leather with a particular appearance and color. That's why it's always a good idea to buy more leather up front than you think you will need.

## WHERE TO PURCHASE YOUR LEATHER

Leather can be bought in specialized shops or online. Shopping in a retail store gives you the advantage of seeing and touching the leather in person. You can bring along your pattern pieces and lay them out directly on the hides to avoid buying too much leather or realizing later that the piece you bought is too small or has blemishes in the wrong spots. Specialized online dealers often give you the option to order samples before you buy. Because the leather tanning process is not always consistent, request samples first and then order from the same batch of leather. You will find a list of manufacturers and suppliers on page 127.

## SOURCING LEATHER AND SUSTAINABILITY

Leather is a fantastic material because it is so durable, which makes it perfectly suited for everyday bags. However, it's important to be mindful of the fact that it is animal skin. It's important to choose producers that practice the humane treatment of animals and source leather from animals that were used in meat production. Leather from Europe, especially Germany, is the best option. A second factor to consider is the environmental impact and sustainability of the leather. Leather has to be tanned to keep it from decomposing, and the tanning process typically involves many chemicals that could be harmful to the environment, workers, and ground water. Leftover chemicals may also be present in the finished leather. I recommend chromium-free leather (also known as chrome-free leather) from Germany. The quality is worth the price.

## LEATHER WEIGHT AND THICKNESS

Leather with a weight of 2–3 ounces (about 1 mm thick) is ideal for working on a home sewing machine. Using leather with a heavier weight can create potential problems. While most home sewing machines can sew one layer of leather without difficulty, most handbag projects require you to sew seams through several layers of leather. This exponentially increases the weight that your sewing machine has to handle. For example, if you use a leather with a weight of 2–3 ounces (1 mm thick), your sewing machine has to handle a weight of at least 5 ounces (2 mm thick) just to sew a basic seam with two layers. At the corners and any other areas where there is a fold, this weight is doubled again—your layers will now have a total weight of 10 ounces (4 mm thick). This can be very difficult for a home sewing machine. Even the best ones gradually reach their limit at weights of more than 10 ounces. For the designs in this book, the number of leather layers that have to be sewn together is kept to a minimum to ensure that the designs can be sewn on regular home sewing machines.

Leatherworkers sometimes use an appliance called a skiving machine to reduce the thickness of a piece of leather. It cuts thin slices along the edges on the unfinished side and, for edges with a seam allowance, can create thinner seams. It is also possible to skive leather manually with a skiving knife or round knife. Skiving is better suited for heavyweight leathers. Other types of leather may tear.

Very fine leathers such as lambskin or goatskin can easily stretch out of shape and, in the worst-case scenario, tear while being sewn. This type of leather is therefore better left for the experts.

## TANNING AND DYEING

Leather is tanned and dyed in batches that consist of several hides, which explains why there can be slight color variation among different batches. Depending on the dye used, the color may not be very lightfast, meaning that it could change or fade when exposed to sunlight. Leather can sometimes also stain or rub onto lighter-colored fabrics. Remember: Pay attention to quality and to the information from the manufacturer to avoid these problems.

## STORING LEATHER

Leather should always be rolled up loosely with the rough side facing outwards. You should never fold your leather. Folds can be pressed into the leather permanently and impossible to remove. Such folds form particularly quickly in coated leather and patent leather. Leather should be stored somewhere that isn't too humid or too dry; make sure the area has adequate ventilation and is away from direct sunlight. For example, it's a good idea to avoid storing leather in a basement.

## TESTING LEATHER

Again, it is always important to test leather on a sewing machine first. How does the leather behave when it is sewn? Does it move through the machine evenly? What is the best stitch length and which thread should be used? These questions are best answered with a test piece. Plus, you'll get comfortable with your material and your machine.

## FAUX LEATHER

Faux leather is available in a variety of finishes. Like fabric, faux leather is sold by the yard. Faux leather can imitate smooth leather, suede, or reptile leather and is frequently made of woven fabric that has been coated with PVC, polyurethane, or a similar material. There are also various types of microfiber fabrics available, such as Alcantara. Because faux leather is not a natural product, it can be considered vegan. Unfortunately, it is not climate-neutral, sustainable, or environmentally friendly because it is an industrial product and many chemicals are used to manufacture it.

Faux leather is often much more affordable but can seldom compete with the characteristics of real leather. It quickly becomes brittle, and its coating can rub off.

One advantage of faux leather is that the material can be produced in practically any color, print, or texture with no irregularities—unless that's part of the design intent.

Compared to types of heavier natural leather, faux leather is also softer and easier to handle on a sewing machine.

Unlike leather, the edges of faux leather cannot be left unfinished, so if you're using faux leather instead of real leather, add a seam allowance so that the edges can be turned under, or finish the edges using your preferred metthod.

Faux leather is often stiffer than real leather, so it is not always suitable for more relaxed and slouchy bag designs. For the same reason, handbags made with faux leather don't require a lining material to give it structure as handbags made with bonded leather would, for example.

## TIP

Just like leather, faux leather should not be pinned together because this would damage the material. Instead, use binder clips and double-sided tape.

FAUX COWHIDE
LEATHER

ALCANTARA®

FAUX REPTILE
LEATHER

FAUX LEATHER WITH
METALLIC FINISH
AND GEOMETRIC
EMBOSSING

# TYPES OF LEATHER

There are several types of leather that are suitable for a home sewing machine. Below is a brief description of some of the different kinds and their characteristics.

## Smooth Leather

This term refers to various leathers that have a smooth surface. One side of the leather is smooth, and the other is rough. The smooth side is usually the top grain side. Smooth leather does not necessarily come from a particular animal and can be made from cowhide, calfskin, or goatskin. Napa leather (see below) also falls in this category.

## Napa Leather

Napa leather is a general term that describes leather that is relatively soft and supple. It is a smooth leather that is most often made from cowhide, but there are also goatskin and lambskin napas. With a maximum weight of 2–3 ounces (0.8–1.2 mm), napa leather is ideal for working with a home sewing machine.

## Cowhide

Cowhide is a collective term for leathers that come from cattle. They can have a variety of textures and appearances. It is often sold in half hides, or sides.

## Leather Strips

Leather strips, such as blank strips for straps and belt blanks, are cut from high-quality leather, typically with a weight of more than 6 ounces (2.5 mm). They are rarely suitable for a home sewing machine, but blank leather strips are the perfect material for sturdy straps. The straps should be secured with rivets rather than being sewn.

## Split Leather

Split leather is leather from the lower layers of a hide. In contrast to smooth leather, it does not retain the layers with the original grain. As a result, a coating is applied, and the split leather is embossed with an imitation grain. Alternatively, split leather can have a buffed surface on both sides. This type of leather is often cheaper than smooth leather.

## Patent Leather

Patent leather has a smooth, glossy surface that has been finished with a varnish. This means that the original grain is no longer visible. Patent leather has almost no elasticity and can be handled on home sewing machines.

## Reptile Leather

Reptile leather encompasses leather produced from fish, lizards, snakes, and crocodiles. When buying reptile leather, it is particularly important to avoid any leather that comes from endangered or protected species. Some reptile leathers can be sustainable if they are produced, for example, from byproducts of the edible fish industry. In most cases, the surface of reptile leather has a typical grain structure, but because the skins are relatively thin and small, they're not worth the money. Reptile grain can also be printed or embossed on other non-reptile leathers.

## Suede

Suede refers to leather with a buffed surface. It is not produced from the top grain, but rather a lower, inner layer of a split hide. Suede frequently has a napped finish on both sides. Velour is a typical example of a suede.

## Velour

Velour is a uniformly soft, velvety leather that is produced from the inner layer of a hide. It has a napped finish and tends to be cheaper than smooth leather.

## Nubuck

Nubuck is created by brushing and buffing the top grain side of a hide. It is a delicate and high-end material.

## Goatskin

Goatskin is generally a very supple and soft leather. Because goats are relatively small, so are their skins. Goatskins are therefore commonly bought as whole hides.

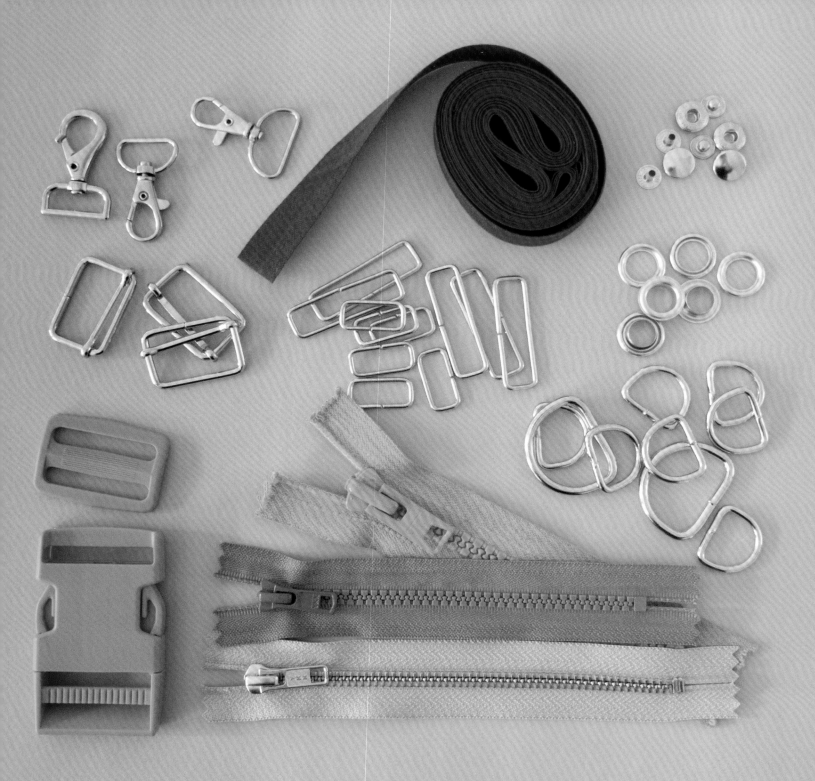

# TOOLS

## METAL RULER
Slightly flexible rulers without a cork backing work best for the projects in this book. I recommend always keeping various sizes of rulers on hand. It's good to have a metal ruler that's at least 20 inches (50 cm) long for larger pattern pieces. For smaller pieces and detail work, a 12-inch (30 cm) ruler is recommended. Plastic rulers should not be used for leatherworking because they can be damaged by the sharp blades of your tools.

## CRAFT KNIVES OR ROTARY CUTTERS WITH REPLACEMENT BLADES
Leather must always be cut exactly to size. For this reason, scissors or a basic utility knife are not suitable, They do not create smooth or precise edges and cannot be used to cut directly along the edges of the pattern. Always use a craft knife or rotary cutter instead, making sure to replace the blades regularly for a consistent, sharp cutting edge. Cutting blades should be replaced regularly and disposed of safely. Wrap up the blades in paper before throwing them away.

## AWLS
An awl is used to transfer markings from a pattern to the leather. Your awl should fit comfortably in your hand and can also be used to pre-punch seams or make small holes.

## CUTTING MAT
Cutting mats can be used to protect your work surface and keep the blades of your craft knife or rotary cutter sharper for a longer period of time. Choose a cutting mat that is at least 12 × 18 inches (31 × 46 cm)—the bigger, the better.

## BONE FOLDER
A bone folder makes it easier to fold leather or shape turned corners, edges, and curves. It can also be used to affix double-sided tape evenly to a piece of leather.

## PENCIL OR TAILOR'S CHALK
To transfer markings from the pattern to the fabric, you can use a regular pencil or tailor's chalk. An extra fine point mechanical pencil is recommended for very precise markings. This ensures that the markings will be covered by a stitch later and will not be visible on the final product.

## BINDER CLIPS
Pins should not be used when working with leather because they will poke permanent holes. Instead, use binder clips to hold your materials together while sewing. Binder clips are available in various sizes. The recommended sizes for working on a home sewing machine are ½ inch to ¾ inch (1.5–2 cm).

## LEATHER HAND NEEDLES AND NEEDLE GRABBER
Leather hand needles for hand sewing usually come in a package containing an assortment of different sizes. Just like leather needles for sewing machines, leather hand needles are wedge-shaped and therefore very sharp. Use a needle grabber to protect your fingertips when you are sewing by hand. These small rubbery discs are made of silicone or a similar material and allows you to firmly grip the needle, which prevents it from slipping, especially when you're working with heavyweight materials and leather. A thimble provides additional protection for your fingertips.

SCHMETZ
LEDER
LEATHER
130/705 H LL
80 80 90 90 100
12 12 14 14 16

131 259

6
Ledernadeln
Leather
needles

No. 3-7

K

Aiguilles pour cuir

ROTARY CUTTER
45 mm

## SCISSORS

Leather should not be cut with scissors. Nevertheless, various types of scissors are essential for working with the other materials used in the projects. Fabric shears are a valuable tool for cutting fabric. A regular pair of household scissors or universal scissors works fine for cutting double-stick tape, masking tape, and other similar items. There are special thread scissors to get a nice clean cut on the ends of threads, and pinking shears are sometimes needed to shorten zippers or trim the seam allowance of a lining. Unlike normal scissors, an edge made with pinking shears won't fray easily.

## ROTARY PUNCH

A rotary punch with different hole punch sizes ranging from $\frac{1}{16}$ to $\frac{13}{64}$ inch (1–4 mm) can be used to punch precise holes for rivets, snap fasteners, or grommets. For belt holes and holes for button studs, a rotary punch is essential because they remain visible in the finished project and should look uniform.

## HOLLOW PUNCH TOOL

Hollow punch tools serve the same purpose as a rotary punch, but they require a mallet to use them. They are available in various diameters ranging from $\frac{1}{16}$ to $\frac{13}{16}$ inch (1–20 mm). The advantage of hollow punch tools is that it can create holes with larger diameters. This makes them particularly useful for punching holes for button studs.

## MALLET

A mallet may be needed to secure rivets, snap fasteners, and grommets to bags. You can also use a mallet to hammer down the thicker areas of a piece of leather.

## SEAM RIPPER

A seam ripper is usually part of the basic equipment that comes with a sewing machine. Leather seams should not be pulled apart, but if you make a mistake when sewing fabric, the seam ripper will help you separate the seams. Be careful not to damage the material in the process.

## IRON AND IRONING BOARD

An iron is used to press fabrics into shape and open seam allowances. Leather should not be ironed because it can shrink when exposed to heat.

## DOUBLE-SIDED TAPE

When working with leather, it's important to use double-sided tape as a substitute for pins to keep everything in place. You can secure pieces of leather before sewing without needing to poke holes and create tidy seams. I recommend narrow double-sided tape with a width between $\frac{3}{16}$ inch and $\frac{1}{4}$ inch (5–6 mm). Tidy seams can also be achieved by brushing the seams with leather or wood glue. If you're using glue, be sure to work in a well-ventilated area.

## MASKING TAPE

Masking tape is used to adhere the pattern piece to the leather. Masking tape commonly comes in a width of $\frac{1}{2}$ inch (13 mm), which will work well with these projects. For more information about cutting leather and using masking tape, see page 27.

## PINS

Pins are used only for sewing fabrics and never for leather. That being said, it is useful to have a few pins on hand for any pieces of fabric that you need to sew.

## SAFETY PINS

Safety pins are used for the designs that have drawstrings. Any size will suffice for these projects.

## OTHER HELPFUL TOOLS

If your leather isn't gliding easily beneath the presser foot of your sewing machine, it helps to place a piece of parchment paper between the leather and the foot. A plastic ruler can be used for the same purpose. If you use a plastic ruler, be careful not to sew through it—always keep it a good distance from the seam. Parchment paper can theoretically be sewn into the seam and ripped away after sewing.

# TECHNIQUES

## WORKING WITH PATTERNS

### LEATHER

All of the patterns in the back of this book include seam allowances measuring ⅜ inch (1 cm) unless otherwise noted. Because leather and faux leather behave consistently (unlike other types of fabric), this seam allowance should suffice. If you choose to use different materials or would like to finish your seams, you should check the seam allowances and adjust them, if necessary. The seams for leather and faux leather are not usually hemmed, meaning the edges remain unfinished.

The pattern pieces also include notches along the edges of the material. You can use the notches to align the pieces correctly. They also indicate the length of the seam allowance.

Every leather hide is unique. This means that there is no right or wrong way to orient the pattern pieces. There is one exception: velour leather. Because the nap may run in a specific direction, you will need to pay attention to the orientation if you use this material.

The pattern pieces should be copied and cut out very carefully, preferably with a craft knife or rotary cutter. First, secure the pattern into place on your piece of leather. Pierce any marking points onto the pattern with an awl or pin. Be sure that you do not poke all the way through the leather; only make light marks. For more detailed step-by-step instructions, see the next page.

### FABRIC

As with the patterns for the leather, the patterns for the fabric pieces are designed with seam allowances. Most of the time, they will not be clipped. Secure the pattern onto the fabric with pattern weights or pins. Trace the outline with a pen and then cut out the fabric with scissors. Pay attention to the grain when cutting fabric. For more detailed step-by-step instructions, see page 29.

### FLEECE INTERFACING OR BATTING

Fleece interfacing is cut in a similar manner to fabric—use pattern weights or pin the pattern to the interfacing. Trace the outline of the patterns with a pen and then cut out the pieces.

## CUTTING LEATHER

Leather should never be cut with scissors. Because the pattern needs to be secured directly onto the leather, you will not be able to cut precisely along the edge with scissors. Plus, you run the risk of cutting the pattern itself. Leather should always be laid flat on a cutting mat.

You will need the following tools to cut your leather: cutting mat, masking tape, craft knife or rotary cutter, and a metal ruler.

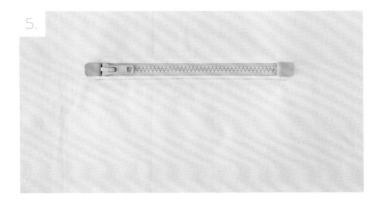

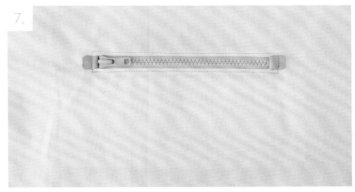

5. Sew from the front along the bottom of the zipper. This is easiest to do with the zipper foot.

6. Fold the inside pocket material along the marked fold line and pin the top edge to the wrong side of the lining, above the zipper.

7. From the front, sew along the top edge of the zipper, making sure that you are sewing the zipper to the fabric of your inside pocket.

8. To close up the sides of the inside pocket, sew from the back along the sides of the pocket.

## METHOD 2: FACING

This method works well for lighter-weight linings and creates a stronger inside edge on the zipper opening. However, with heavier fabrics, the edge could end up being too thick.

Patterns:
1.3.5 IT Inside Pocket (1 × lining material)
1.3.5 BE Inside Pocket Facing (1 × lining material)

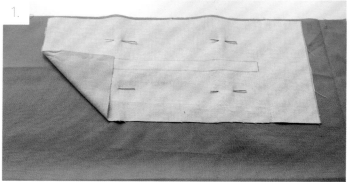

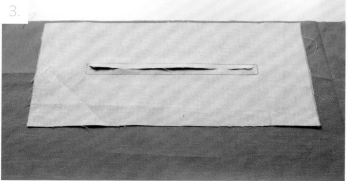

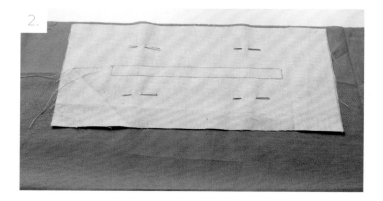

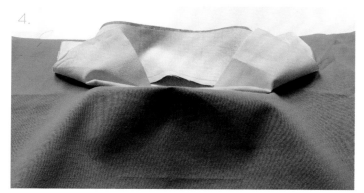

1. Cut the fabric for the lining of your bag with the appropriate pattern piece and transfer the markings for the zipper opening. Pin the facing to the front of the lining, aligning the markings with the zipper opening exactly. The right sides of both pieces of fabric should face each other.

2. Sew a rectangle along the outlines of the zipper opening.

3. With a craft knife, cut through the middle of the sewn rectangle and diagonally into the corners.

4. Pull the facing through the opening to the wrong side of the lining. Press the opening flat and then continue with Step 3 of Method 1.

# ATTACHING RIVETS, GROMMETS, SNAP FASTENERS, AND BUTTON STUDS

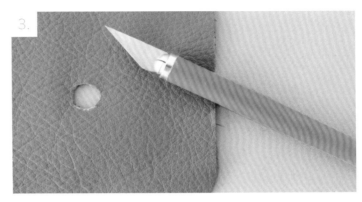

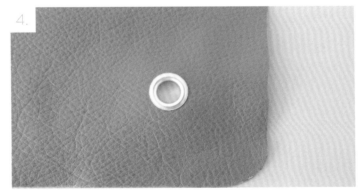

The cutting and punching tools that come with rivets, snap fasteners, and grommets are often not very sharp (1). As a result, they are often unsuitable for leatherwork. Instead of struggling with a dull tool, I recommend using it to mark the area to be cut (2). Then, make a cut with a craft knife or rotary punch, using the marking as a guide (3).

5.

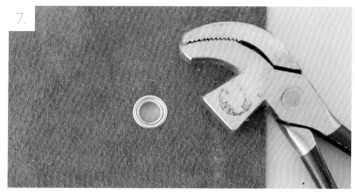

7.

6.

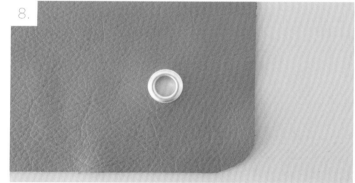

8.

The hole for rivets, button studs, and snap fasteners should always be made as small as possible to keep the metal parts from moving around (4–6). If you are attaching lots of rivets or studs, you should consider investing in a pair of special pliers, such as those made by Prym (7). The different dies that come with rivets, grommets, or snap fasteners can be inserted into the pliers, making the work of attaching the metal pieces precise, easy, and tidy (8).

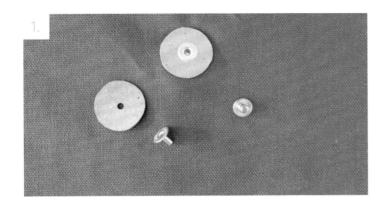

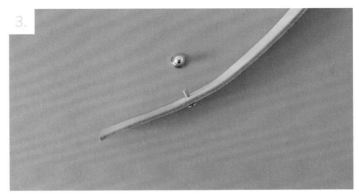

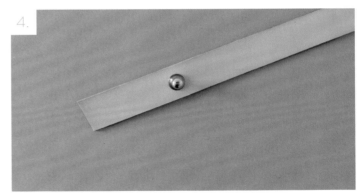

When you attach snap fasteners to fabric, the fabric may rip if you use the fasteners frequently. It's best to use only an awl to puncture the fabric instead of a rotary punch or the punching tool that comes with the fasteners. This way, the fabric will be less likely to rip or become damaged. Before puncturing the fabric, you can reinforce it by ironing a small piece of fusible interfacing to the reverse side of the fabric or by inserting a disc of bonded leather when you attach the snap fastener. It is a good idea to reinforce faux leather in this way as well (1).

To use button studs to join two straps, punch a very small hole into one of the straps with your rotary hole punch, poke the base piece through the hole, and screw the stud onto the base piece (2–4). No hardware is required for the other strap. All you need to do is punch a hole that is just large enough for the stud to enter through it. If the punch of your rotary hole punch is not large enough, you can enlarge the hole by cutting a small vertical slit off on one side. When attaching snaps, button studs, rivets, and grommets, always remember to do a test run with a scrap piece of leather before you work on your finished piece.

## ATTACHING STRAPS

When attaching straps, it's important to make sure that they don't get twisted. The same side of both ends of the straps should be sewn or riveted onto the bag.

Depending on what material you use for a strap, the ends may need to be sealed to prevent them from fraying or unraveling. For example, the ends of polyester straps can be sealed using a lighter. The ends of cotton webbing must be tucked under or covered with another material, such as a small piece of leather.

The seams that secure the straps to your bag are frequently put under heavy strain, so it's a good idea to reinforce them. There are different methods for reinforcing a seam. For example, the straps can be secured by sewing a square with an "X" through it, which is called a "Box X" stitch. In addition or as an alternative, the seams can be reinforced by sewing a lockstitch into the corners.

Depending on their thicknesses, leather straps can be difficult to sew on home sewing machines. I recommend attaching them with rivets instead (see page 37).

Always remember to attach the straps to a test scrap first before working on your final piece.

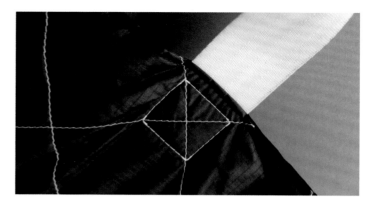

PIPING ON THE AHLBECK BUCKET BAG

## SEWING LEATHER BY HAND

A special leather or triangular point needle is recommended for sewing leather by hand. Be careful: Triangular point needles are very sharp! It's a good idea to always have a thimble or needle grabber on hand. Hand-sewing leather can be fairly difficult because it's not easy to pierce the leather with the tip of the needle. However, the holes can be pre-punched with an awl. There are also special tools made for punching several holes at the same time. They also make it easy to maintain the distance between your punched holes, which means the stitch length stays consistent and the finished seam looks nice and uniform. Hand-sewing is hard on your hands and fingers, and you may find that it causes blisters.

## JOINING THE ENDS OF BIAS TAPE

Although this technique is not directly related to leatherworking, joining bias tape ends does come up in this book. The method shown here is a little cumbersome, but it results in neat and tidy seams and ends. This is particularly advantageous if you are using a bias tape in a contrasting color.

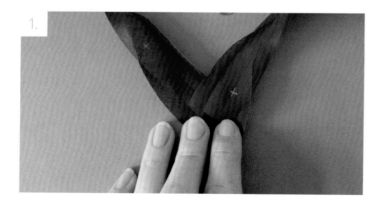

1. Clip the bias tape to the open edge of your bag using binder clips. On the back sides of each piece of bias tape, measure and mark the exact length that you want. Make your mark in the center of the bias tape rather than on the edges.

2. Draw a diagonal line at a 45° angle from the edge of the bias tape. The line should run through the marks at the center of the bias tape. Draw a second parallel line ¼ inch (6 mm) from the first line on the side near the end of the bias tape. Repeat for the other piece of bias tape.

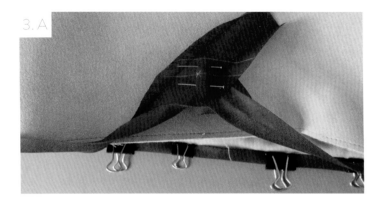

3. A

4.

3. B

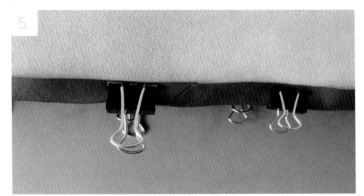

5.

3. Pin the pieces of bias tape together on top of each other, right sides together. Make sure that the lines and the center marks are lined up (A). Sew the pieces together along the line with the center mark (B).

4. Unfold the bias tape and cut along the second line to trim the extra fabric.

5. Fold and press the edges toward the center of the bias strip to make one continuous strip. Place the bias tape neatly along the edge of your project. The edges of the bias tape should butt up against each other perfectly. Sew the bias tape onto the bag.

# BEFORE YOU START

Test, test, test! Before you get started, it's important to test each step first. Choose a simple sewing project to start with. This will give you a feel for the work. Familiarize yourself with the material and how it behaves with your cutting tools. Practice cutting with your craft knife or rotary cutter as straight and precisely as you can.

Make sure your workspace has adequate lighting and a comfortable place to cut your fabric, so you don't hurt your back. Leather and fabric are easiest to cut while standing. Most tables are a little too low for this. If you have the option to use an elevated cutting table that is the same height as a kitchen counter, your back will thank you. Always use a cutting mat. This will protect the surface of your table and help keep your blades sharp.

Pay attention to your seam allowances. To sew a consistent seam allowance, you can follow the markings on your sewing machine or use washi tape. Measure the correct distance from the needle and affix a piece of tape to the sewing machine at the correct seam allowance. It can be

removed without leaving a residue. For more information about sewing a consistent seam allowance, see the Glossary on page 120.

Use the right thread for the needle thread and bobbin. Thread your machine and test the settings. Before you begin, prepare your material and make sure you have all the accessories you will need. It's especially helpful to have plenty of replacement blades on hand for your craft knife or rotary cutter.

Leather is probably one of the thickest materials you will ever work with on your home sewing machine. When you start your first stitch, you might find that the foot does not initially glide over the leather. You can avoid this problem by creating a small wedge. Sew two to three layers of leather together and slide the wedge beneath the back edge of the presser foot. This allows the sewing machine to sew "uphill" and feed the fabric more easily.

# PATTERN KEY

A: Flap, closure, outer-

AH: Handle

AT: Outside of bag

B: Base

BE: Facing

HR: D-ring holder

I: Inner-

IT: Inside pocket

O: Top

PA: Padding cover

P: Padding

R: Zipper, back

RA: Zipper cover

RU: Curve

S: Side

SL: Loop

ST: Strap template

T: Bag

U: Bottom

V: Front

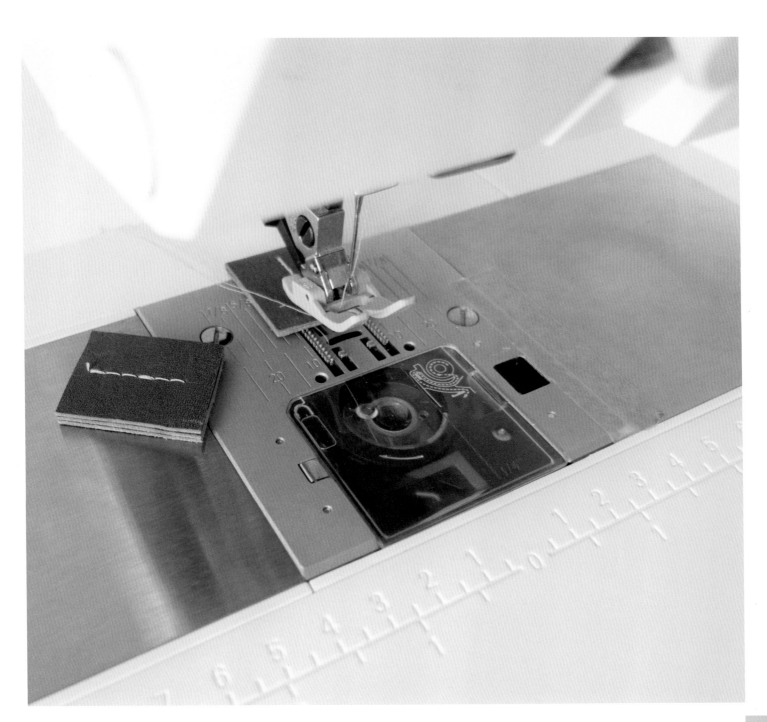

# The Eldena 1C
## Tote

A SPACIOUS SHOULDER BAG FOR AN OUTING IN THE CITY OR A DAY AT THE BEACH.

The straps for this version of the Eldena are made of sturdy leather and attached with rivets. Leather-reinforced corners give the bag more strength and make a bold statement.

**LEVEL: INTERMEDIATE**

## MATERIALS

1⅜ square feet (0.12 m²) of leather or ¼ yard (18 cm) of faux leather

⅝ yard (55 cm) of canvas (7–9 ounces or 240–320 g/m²), washed in cold water

⅝ yard (55 cm) of lining material, such as lightweight cotton (4–5 ounces or 100–180 g/m²), washed in cold water

1-inch (2.5 cm) wide leather strap, 54 inches (136 cm) long

8 tubular rivets

#5 closed-end zipper, 6¼ inches (16 cm) long

## TOOLS

Paper, pen, masking tape, and scissors for the patterns

Sewing machine, needles, and thread

Craft knife

Awl

Metal ruler

Double-sided tape

Binder clips

Pins

Iron and ironing board

Rotary punch

Mallet (for attaching the grommets)

Edge-stitch foot (optional)

## PATTERN PIECES (Pattern Sheet A)

**Canvas**

2 × 2.1C AVR Eldena 1C Tote Front and Back

**Leather or Faux Leather**

4 × 2.1C AVRU Eldena 1C Tote Corner Reinforcement

**Lining Material**

2 × 2.1 IVR Eldena Tote Front and Back

1 × 1.3.5 IT Inside Pocket

1 × 1.3.5 BE Inside Pocket Facing (optional)

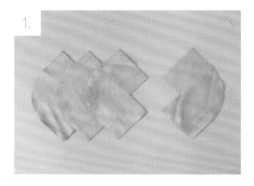

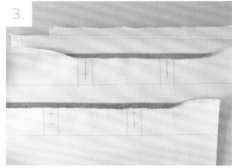

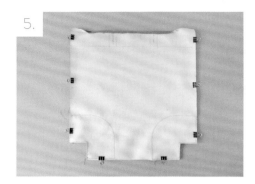

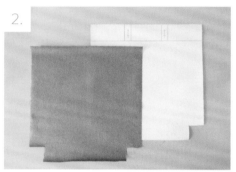

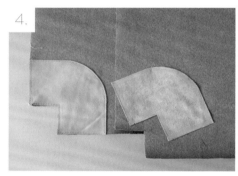

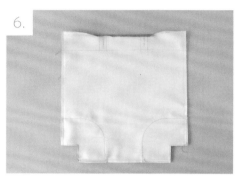

1. Cut the four corner reinforcements from the leather. Transfer the pattern markings to the leather.

2. Cut the front and back pieces from the canvas and the front, back, and inside pocket pieces from the lining material. Transfer the pattern markings for the straps to the canvas. Transfer the markings for the zipper to one of the lining pieces.

3. Press back the top edges and sides of the canvas front and back pieces along the seam allowance. Repeat for the lining pieces.

4. Place the leather corner reinforcements on top of the cutout corners of the bottom of the front and back pieces, making sure the notches in the straight edges are lined up. Using double-sided tape, affix the reinforcements to the canvas. The wrong side of the leather should be facing the right side of the canvas. Sew the leather pieces onto the canvas about ⅛ inch (3 mm) from the edge of the leather.

5. Prepare to sew the front and back pieces of the canvas together. Lay one canvas piece on top of the other, right sides together. Unfold the top seam allowance. Use binder clips to hold the pieces together.

6. Sew the front and back pieces together along the seam allowance markings. For now, sew only the left, right, and bottom sides. Leave the cutout corners open.

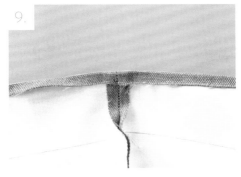

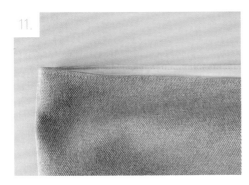

7. To sew the corners of the bag, push the side and bottom edges of the joined canvas and leather piece together until the side seams are perpendicular to the bottom seams. Sew along the open edges (Photo 8). When you finish sewing, turn the bag right side out.

To avoid sewing through too many layers of leather, it's a good idea to carefully fold back the top and side seam allowances or even tape them back with double-sided tape. The best way to do this is to fold the side seam allowance to the left and the bottom seam allowance to the right. The seams will automatically fit together.

8. Create the lining. You may need to switch the thread in your machine for this step. Sew the inside zipper pocket (pages 29–32). Then sew the front and back lining pieces together. The right sides of the pieces should face each other. Just like the outside of the bag, sew only the left, right, and bottom sides together. Sew the corners of the lining together, as described in Step 7.

9. Fold back and tape the seam allowances on the side edges of the joined canvas piece and lining. Then fold and tape the seam allowance on the top edge of the bag over the folded seam allowances on the sides.

10. Now you will sew the parts of the bag together. You may need to switch threads for this. Place the lining in the bag, wrong sides together. Starting on one side, align the side seam of the lining with the side seam of the canvas bag. Use binder clips, pins, or double-sided tape to secure the top edges of the lining to the canvas.

11. To sew the canvas to the lining, carefully topstitch along the top of your bag ⅛ inch (3 mm) from the edge, using a ⅛-inch (3 mm) edge-stitch foot if you have one.

12. Using the pattern markings, attach the straps to the bag with rivets (page 37).

# The Eldena 1D Tote

A SLEEK TONE-ON-TONE
VARIATION OF THE
ELDENA.

With a faux leather base, this tote is
a slightly less expensive alternative.

**LEVEL: INTERMEDIATE**

## MATERIALS

½ yard (35 cm) faux leather

½ yard (40 cm) of 100% polyester canvas fabric (7–9 ounces or 240–320 g/m²)

⅝ yard (55 cm) of lining material, such as lightweight cotton (4–5 ounces or 100–180 g/m²), washed in cold water

1½ yards (136 cm) of webbing, 1½ inches (40 mm) wide

#5 closed-end zipper, 6¼ inches (16 cm) long

## TOOLS

Paper, pen, masking tape, and scissors for the patterns

Sewing machine, needles, and thread

Craft knife

Awl

Metal ruler

Double-sided tape

Binder clips

Pins

Iron and ironing board

Edge-stitch foot (optional)

## PATTERN PIECES (Pattern Sheet A)

**Canvas**

2 × 2.1D AVRO Eldena 1D Tote Top Front and Back

**Faux Leather**

2 × 2.1D AVRU Eldena 1D Tote Bottom Front and Back

**Lining Material**

2 × 2.1 IVR Eldena Tote Lining Front and Back

1 × 1.3.5 IT Inside Pocket

1 × 1.3.5 BE Inside Pocket Facing (optional)

## VARIATION

Make this bag your own! Feel free to use webbing with a different width or try a different method to attach the straps. The straps can be secured on the outside or inside of the bag and attached by sewing or with rivets. For more information on attaching straps, see page 36.

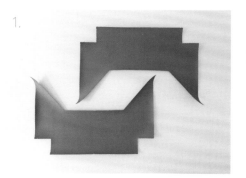

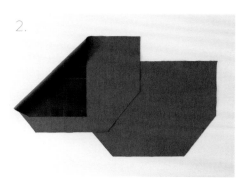

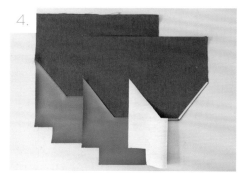

1. Cut the front and back bottom pieces of the faux leather to size. Transfer the pattern markings to the wrong side of the leather.

2. Cut the front and back pieces from the canvas and the front, back, and inside pocket pieces from the lining material. Transfer the pattern markings for the straps to the canvas. Transfer the pattern markings for the zipper to one of the lining pieces.

3. Press back the top edges and sides of the canvas front and back pieces along the seam allowance. Repeat for the lining pieces.

4. Tape the top edges of each faux leather piece to the bottom edges of each canvas piece with double-sided tape. The wrong side of the leather should be facing the right side of the canvas. Stitch each faux leather piece to the canvas about ⅛ inch (3 mm) from the edge. The seams will be invisible on the outside and inside of the finished bag.

5. Prepare to sew the front and back pieces of the canvas together. Lay one canvas piece on top of the other, right sides together. Unfold the top seam allowance. Use binder clips to hold the pieces together.

6. Sew the front and back pieces together along the seam allowances. For now, sew only the left, right, and bottom sides. Leave the corners open.

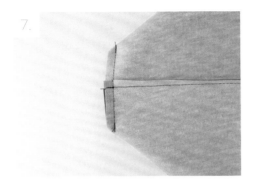

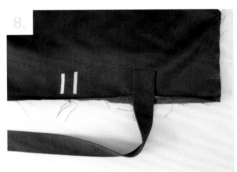

7. To sew the corners of the bag, push the side and bottom edges of the joined canvas and leather piece together until the side seams are perpendicular to the bottom seams. Sew along the open edges (Photo 8). When you finish sewing, turn the bag right side out.

To avoid sewing through too many layers of leather, it's a good idea to carefully fold back the top and side seam allowances or even tape them back with double-sided tape. The best way to do this is to fold the side seam allowance to the left and the bottom seam allowance to the right. The seams will automatically fit together.

8. Using the pattern markings, attach the straps to the back. (For more information, see the detailed instructions on page 36.)

9. Create the lining. You may need to switch the thread in your machine for this step. Sew the inside zipper pocket (pages 29–32). Then lay the front lining piece on top of the bottom lining piece. The right sides of the pieces should face each other. Just like the outside of the bag, sew only the left, right, and bottom sides together. Sew the corners of the lining together, as described in Step 7.

10. Fold back and tape the seam allowances on the side edges of the joined canvas piece and lining. Then fold and tape the seam allowance on the top edge of the bag over the folded seam allowances on the sides.

11. Now you will sew the parts of the bag together. You may need to switch threads for this. Place the lining in the bag, wrong sides together. Starting on one side, align the side seam of the lining with the side seam of the canvas bag. Use binder clips, pins, or double-sided tape to secure the top edges of the lining to the canvas.

12. To sew the canvas to the lining, carefully topstitch along the top seam of your bag ⅛ inch (3 mm) from the edge, using a ⅛-inch (3 mm) edge-stitch foot if you have one.

# The Seby Clutch

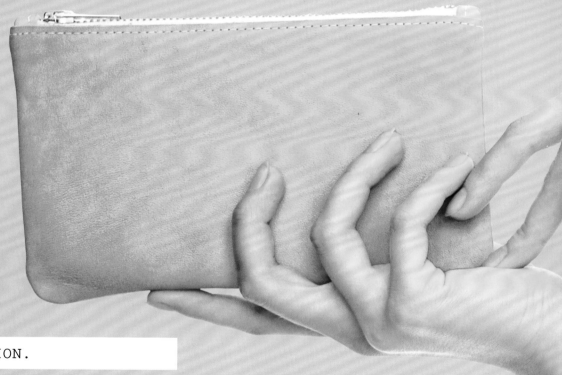

This compact clutch can be used as a cosmetic bag or wallet. You can slip it easily inside another handbag. This is a small, moderately difficult sewing project that relies on precision.

**LEVEL: INTERMEDIATE**

## MATERIALS

1 piece of leather, about 12 × 8¾ inches (30 × 22 cm)

1 piece of lining material, such as lightweight cotton (4–5 ounces or 100–180 g/m²), about 11⅞ × 8¾ inches (30 × 22 cm) or 5⅞ × 17¾ inches (15 × 45 cm), washed in cold water

#5 closed-end zipper, 6¼ inches (16 cm) long

## TOOLS

Paper, pen, masking tape, and scissors for the patterns

Sewing machine, needles, and thread

Craft knife

Awl

Metal ruler

Double-sided tape

Binder clips

Pins

Iron and ironing board (optional)

Zipper foot (optional)

Pinking shears (to trim the zipper)

## PATTERN PIECES (Pattern Sheet A)

### Leather

2 × 2.2 VR Seby Clutch Front and Back

2 × 2.2 RA Seby Clutch Zipper End Cover

### Lining Material

2 × 2.2 VR Seby Clutch Front and Back

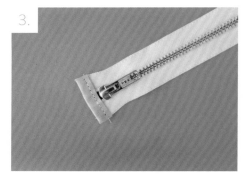

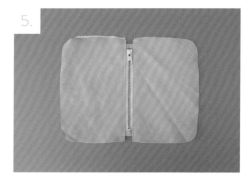

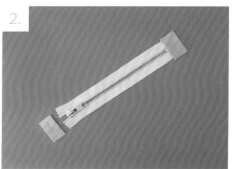

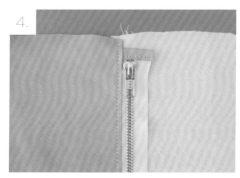

1. Cut the front and back pieces and the zipper end covers from the leather and the front and back pieces from the lining. Transfer the pattern markings for the beginning and end of the seam to the wrong side of the lining.

2. Prepare to sew the leather zipper end covers. To ensure that the covers fold over the ends of the zipper properly, use pinking shears to trim slightly under ⅜-inch (1 cm) from each end. Tape each leather piece to each trimmed end.

3. Fold the leather covers over the zipper ends. Make sure that the edges on the topside and underside of the zipper match up perfectly. Tape the back sides of your folded leather covers to the underside of the zipper. Sew the open edges of the leather pieces and the zipper ends together. This is easiest to do with a zipper foot.

4. Next, attach the zipper to the front piece of the leather and the lining. Tape the zipper under the top edge of the leather, right sides facing up. Lay the top edge of the lining under the zipper and secure it with double-sided tape. The right side of the lining piece should also be facing up. Sew the leather, zipper, and lining together ⅛ inch (3 mm) from the edge of the leather, preferably with a zipper foot.

5. Repeat Step 4 to sew the zipper to the back pieces of the leather and the lining.

6. Open the zipper. Lay the two pieces of leather out to one side with the right sides together. Secure them with binder clips. Lay the pieces of lining out to the other side. Line up the edges of the lining and pin them, if necessary. Sew all the edges of the leather with a seam allowance of about 5/16 inch (8 mm). Sew the left and right edges of the lining along the pattern markings with the same seam allowance. Leave the bottom of the lining open for now. Again, this process is easier if you use a zipper foot. To prevent the zipper from getting in the way of your sewing, point the open side of the foot inward, away from the outer edges.

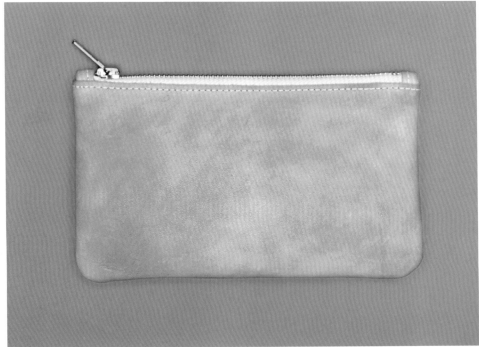

7. For cleaner looking curves around the bottom of the clutch, trim the seam allowance along the rounded corners to about ⅛ inch (3 mm) from the edge of the leather.

8. Turn the outer part of the clutch right side out. Leave the lining inside out. At the bottom of the lining, fold and pin the bottom seam allowance and topstich along the open seam. Tuck the lining back inside the clutch.

TIP
Before you begin, it's a good idea to practice sewing ⅛ inch (3 mm) seam allowances on a scrap piece of leather. The main seam of the clutch is always visible and looks much nicer if it is sewn evenly all the way around.

VARIATION
You can make this clutch in different sizes by scaling the pattern up or down as much as you want. And don't scale the zipper end cover piece—it should stay the same.

# The Rewal
## Drawstring Bag

THE IDEAL BAG FOR CYCLISTS
THAT CAN ALSO BE USED AS A
RUCKSACK.

The Rewal comes together quickly and is a great way for beginners to get comfortable with their sewing machines. Wool felt with leather and thick cotton cord is a perfect combination for fall and winter.

**LEVEL: EASY**

19.

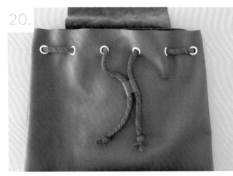

20.

## TIP
The back cushion should be reasonably supportive but still feel soft. You can find suitable material in stores where orthopedic supplies are sold or use a camping mat or sleeping pad.

# The Ahlbeck
## Bucket Bag

A BAG THAT'S IN ITS ELEMENT ON A SUMMER
VACATION, AT THE PARK, OR IN A CAFE.

The sophisticated material used for this bucket bag creates a nice
contrast to the smooth leather straps. The bag has adjustable straps
and can be tossed over a shoulder or worn as a crossbody.

**LEVEL: ADVANCED**

# The Liseby
## Tablet Sleeve and
## the Karleby
## Smartphone Case

FOR DAY-TO-DAY ELEGANCE.

These designs use leather with a woven elastic band, which can also be sewn with contrast stitching. The patterns in this book were designed for tablets that are about 9½ inches tall (24 cm) and 6½ inches (17 cm) wide and for smartphones that are about 5½ inches (14 cm) and 2¾ inches wide (7 cm). However, you can adapt the pattern by measuring the width, depth, and height of your device or using your device as a template.

**LEVEL: EASY**

# The Liseby Tablet Sleeve

## MATERIALS

1 piece of leather, about 15 × 9⅞ inches (38 × 25 cm)*

Woven elastic band, about 19 inches (48 cm) long*

* The exact dimensions of each material will depend on the size of your tablet.

# The Karleby Smartphone Case

## MATERIALS

1 piece of leather, about 7 × 6⅜ inches (17 × 16 cm)*

Woven elastic band, about 12 inches (30 cm) long*

* The exact dimensions of each material will depend on the size of your smartphone.

## TOOLS FOR BOTH

Paper, pen, masking tape, and scissors for the patterns

Masking tape

Sewing machine, needles, and thread

Craft knife

Metal ruler

Awl

Double-sided tape

Binder clips

Edge-stitch foot (optional)

Leather sole and heel edge dressing (for shoe repair)

## PATTERN PIECES (Pattern Sheet C)

**Leather**

2 × 2.8A VR Liseby Tablet Sleeve Front and Back

**Or**

2 × 2.8B VR Karleby Smartphone Case Front and Back

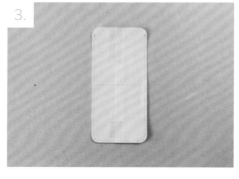

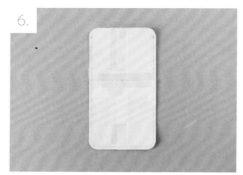

1. If needed, calculate the initial measurements for your customized pattern. Your adjusted pattern should have roughly the following dimensions. For the width, add the following measurements: width of your device + depth of your device + ⅜ inch (8 mm). For the height, add the following measurements: height of your device + ½ the depth of your device + ⅜ inch (8 mm).

2. Alternatively, use your phone as a template to create the adjusted pattern. To adjust the width of the pattern, cut the pattern in half along the vertical markings. Slide the pieces of the pattern around until the width of your smartphone or tablet fits within the edges. Always leave a little extra space near the edges to account for the depth of your device.

3. Tape the two halves together once you have determined the correct width. If your phone is larger than the original pattern, place a bit of extra paper between the two pieces and then tape them together with masking tape.

4. To adjust the height of the pattern, cut the pattern in half along the horizontal markings.

5. Slide the pieces of the pattern around until the height of your device fits within the edges. Again, leave a little extra space at the top and bottom edges of your pattern.

6. Tape the pattern together, as described in Step 3.

7. Cut the leather to size. Transfer the markings for the beginning and end of the seams. For even edges, use a fresh, sharp blade when cutting.

8. Calculate the length of the elastic band. The band should be twice as long as the height of the case. You can also measure the length with your device. Lay your tablet or smartphone in the unfinished case and wrap the piece of elastic band around both items. Adjust the length of the band until it is stretched snugly, but not too tightly, around your device. Because the band will be sewn into the bottom of the case, add an extra ¼-inch (6 mm) to each end to account for the seam allowances. Cut the band to size.

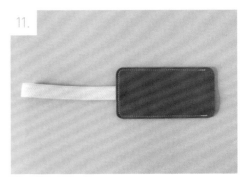

9. Affix double-sided tape to the wrong side of the front piece of leather along the sides and the bottom. Place both ends of the elastic band between the front and back pieces of leather, wrong sides facing out. They can be placed anywhere along the bottom edge of your case. Use a little of masking tape to keep it from sliding when you sew.

10. Peel off the back of the double-sided tape. Tape the front piece on top of the back piece, wrong sides together.

11. Carefully sew along the pattern markings ⅛ inch (3 mm) from the edge, stitching over the elastic band at the bottom.

12. To make the edges a little more durable, you can apply leather edge dressing.

## VARIATION

The case can be lined with felt to create a soft surface for your screen. Use the front and back patterns to cut the felt to size. Place the felt on the leather front piece, wrong sides together. Felt can slide around easily when sewing, so carefully tape it to the leather before you begin your work.

## TIPS

Double check the dimensions of the pattern on your own smartphone or tablet before you cut the leather. Your case will fit pretty snugly at first, but it will stretch out over time.

Woven elastic band is available in fabric and sewing supplies stores. It looks a little nicer than regular elastic band and usually lasts longer as well.

# The Dänholm

## Backpack

MADE FOR YOUR NEXT WEEKEND GETAWAY.

This sewing project is not especially laborious, but its success depends on precise cutting and a clean finish. The reward is a bag that transforms you into a stylish traveler.

**LEVEL: ADVANCED**

## MATERIALS

Approximately 3¼ square feet (0.3 m²) of leather

½ yard (40 cm) of canvas (about 7–9 ounces or 240–320 g/m²), washed in cold water

⅝ yard (50 cm) of lining material, such as lightweight cotton (4–5 ounces or 100–180 g/m²), washed in cold water

½ yard (45 cm) of fleece interfacing

#5 closed-end zipper, 6¼ inches (16 cm) long

2¼ yards (200 cm) of cotton cord

14 grommets, ½ inch (15 mm) in diameter

1 D-ring, 1 inch (25 mm) in diameter

1 snap faster

## TOOLS

Paper, pen, masking tape, and scissors for the patterns

Sewing machine, needles, and thread

Craft knife

Awl

Metal ruler

Double-sided tape

Binder clips

Edge-stitch foot (optional)

Mallet (for attaching the grommets)

Pins

Iron and ironing board

## PATTERN PIECES (Pattern Sheet C)

**Canvas**

2 × 2.9 AVRM Dänholm Backpack Front and Back

**Leather**

2 × 2.9 AVRU Dänholm Backpack Bottom Front and Back

1 × 2.9 AVO Dänholm Backpack Front Top

1 × 2.9 ARO Dänholm Backpack Back Top

1 × 2.9 AB Dänholm Backpack Base

1 × 2.9 ATT Dänholm Backpack Outside Pocket

1 × 2.9 ATA Dänholm Backpack Outside Pocket Flap

1 × 2.9 HR Dänholm Backpack D-ring Loop

**Lining Material**

1 × 2.9 AB Dänholm Backpack Base

2 × 2.9 IVR Dänholm Backpack Lining Front and Back

1 × 1.3.5 IT Inside Pocket

1 × 1.3.5 BE Inside Pocket Facing (optional)

**Fleece Interfacing**

2 × 2.9 VVR Dänholm Backpack Interfacing Front and Back

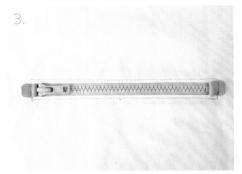

1. Cut the leather, canvas, and lining material pieces. Transfer the pattern markings to the wrong sides of the cut pieces. The markings for the outside pocket should only be transferred to the front piece of the canvas.

2. Press the top seam allowance on the front and back pieces of the lining.

3. Make the inside pocket and sew it to the back lining piece (pages 29–32).

4. Sew the front piece to the back piece, right sides together. Sew only the side and bottom seams to start. Unfold the creased seam allowance at the top and then sew along the edge.

5. Fold the top seam allowance down again and secure it with binder clips.

6. Pin the base lining piece to the bottom of the joined lining piece. The right sides should face inward. Use the notches on the edges of each piece to help you position the base correctly. Sew on the base. The lining is finished!

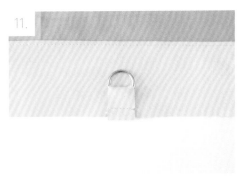

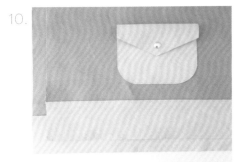

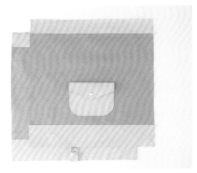

7. Lay the front piece of interfacing on top of the bottom piece. Sew the sides together. Leave the top and bottom open.

8. Using the pattern markings as a guide, attach the snap fastener to both parts of the outside pocket according to the package instructions. Make sure you attach the correct part of the fastener to the correct part of the pocket. The visible part of the snap should be attached to the outside of the flap. (For more information on attaching snap fasteners, see pages 33–35.)

9. And now for the leather. You may need to change your needle, presser foot, and stitch length for this part. Tape the pocket and flap to the front of the canvas piece and stitch both pieces in place. The right side of the pocket fabric should face outwards. Topstitch the side and bottom edges of the pocket along the pattern markings. Leave the top open. Place the flap in the open position with the right side facing the canvas. Sew a single seam parallel to the bottom edge of the flap, as shown in the pattern markings.

10. Secure the leather front and back pieces for the bottom of the bag to the canvas pieces using double-sided tape. Topstitch the leather in place.

11. To attach the D-ring loop to the back piece, first fold the loop in half crosswise over a D-ring. Sew the edges of the loop closed. Secure the D-ring holder to the back piece with double-sided tape.

12. Tape the leather front and back pieces for the top of the backpack to the canvas front and back pieces. Make sure that the correct ones are taped together. Topstitch the leather top pieces to the corresponding canvas pieces.

13.

15.

17.

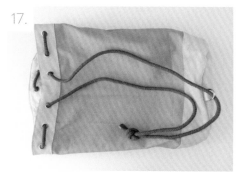

14.

16.

18.

**13.** The front and back pieces can now be sewn together. Place the front piece on top of the back piece, wrong sides together. Make sure that the edges of the leather match up perfectly with each other. For now, sew only the sides.

**14.** Use binder clips to secure the base to the bottom of the front and back pieces. To avoid sewing through several layers of leather, fold open the seam allowances on the sides of the bag. You can keep them in place with double-sided tape. Use the notches on the edges of each piece to help you position the base correctly. Sew the leather base to the finished front and back pieces. Then turn the bag right side out.

**15.** Fold the seam allowances along the top edge of the bag flat. Tape them with double-sided tape. Place the interfacing and lining into the bag and secure the three layers together with double-sided tape or binder clips. The inside pocket should be on the back side of the backpack. Handle the bag gently at this point.

**16.** From the outside, carefully topstitch the top seam to join all three layers.

**17.** Attach the grommets according to the package instructions. (For tips on attaching grommets, see pages 33–34.)

**18.** Thread the cord through the D-ring, and pull it up into the middle grommet in the back of the backpack. Weave the cord through the grommets all the way around the top of the bag and then back through the D-ring. Knot the two cord ends together.

## TIP

It can be difficult to join the layers of leather, interfacing, and lining, so try working on a sample piece first to determine the best needle, thread, and presser foot for the job.

# The Sibby
## Tassel

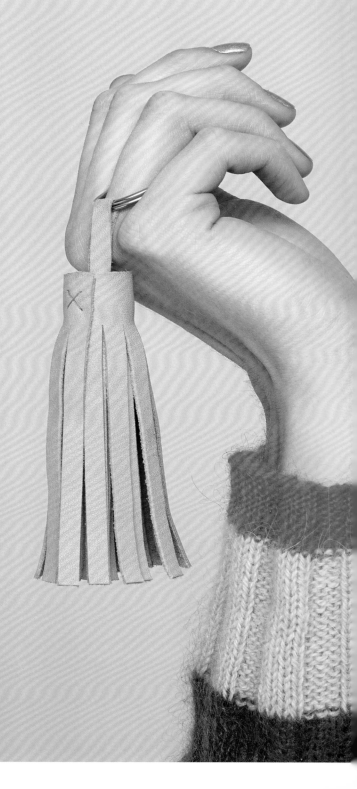

A FASHIONABLE ADDITION TO ANY BAG,
WHETHER AS A KEY CHAIN OR A HANDBAG
CHARM.

No sewing machine is required to make the tassel—
perfect if you're new to leatherworking. It's an excellent
way to use leftover leather.

**LEVEL: EASY**

## MATERIALS

1 piece of leather or faux leather, about 11 × 4 inches
(28 × 10 cm)

1 key ring

## TOOLS

Paper, pen, masking tape, and scissors for the patterns

Leather hand needle and thread

Thimble or needle grabber (optional)

Craft knife

Metal ruler

Awl

Double-sided tape

Hand sewing needle

Key ring

## PATTERN PIECES (Pattern Sheet B)

**Leather or Faux Leather**

1 × 2.10 VR Sibby Tassel

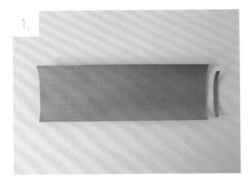

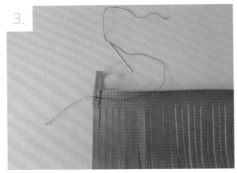

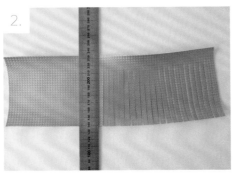

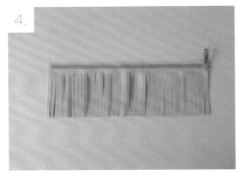

1. Cut the leather rectangle and the leather strip. With an awl, transfer all the pattern markings for the fringe to the cut pieces.

2. Using the markings on the leather rectangle as a guide, carefully cut the individual pieces of fringe.

3. Fold the leather strip in half crosswise and hand-sew it to the marking on the fringed rectangle.

4. Put a piece of double-sided tape on the wrong side of the leather along the long, uncut edge.

5. Peel the back off the tape and carefully roll up the leather rectangle. Start on the side with the loop for the key ring.

6. Once the tassel has been rolled up, use an awl to pierce the markings on the end of the rolled-up piece of leather. The goal here is to transfer the markings to the layer of leather underneath.

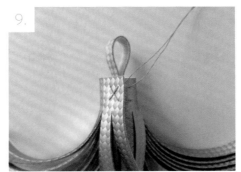

7. The tassel needs a stitch in addition to the double-sided tape to make it nice and strong for repeated use. Unroll the tassel slightly and sew the stitch inside the pierced markings. The stitch will be hidden from view in the finished tassel. Because the tassel is too thick to be sewn on a sewing machine, continue sewing by hand.

8. Roll up the tassel again. Push your leather needle and thread all the way through the tassel several times to stabilize it. This part doesn't require very precise or clean sewing because it will be covered up in the next step.

9. Finish with a decorative stitch. This one is also sewn by hand. Starting from the wrong side of the leather, carefully pull your needle through two layers of leather and form an "X." Knot the thread and hide the knot inside the layers of leather.

10. Attach the key ring to the loop.

## VARIATION

The pattern can be scaled to your preference if you want to make larger tassels or tassels with different proportions.

## TIP

When you cut the fringe, the leather can slip under the metal ruler and cause your fringe to be uneven. To keep the leather in place, hold the ruler down tightly, especially at the ends.

# The Nida
# Luggage Tag

MAKE YOUR LUGGAGE STAND OUT FROM THE
CROWD.

You can use leftover leather pieces in different colors. The
pocket on the front is designed for a 3½ × 2–inch (85 × 55
mm) business card.

**LEVEL: EASY**

## MATERIALS

1 scrap piece of leather, about 9½ × 4¾ inches (24 × 12 cm)

1 leather strip, about 10½–40 inches long (30–100 cm)

## TOOLS

Paper, pen, masking tape, and scissors for the patterns

Sewing machine, needles, and thread

Craft knife

Metal ruler

Awl

Double-sided tape

Rotary punch

## PATTERN PIECES (Pattern Sheet C)

**Leather**

2 × 2.11 AVR Nida Luggage Tag Front and Back

2 × 2.11 AF Nida Luggage Tag Pocket

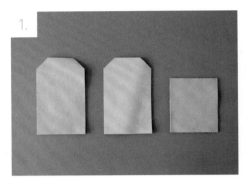

1.

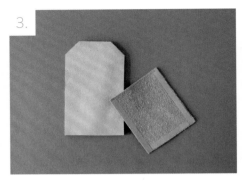

2.

3.

4.

5.

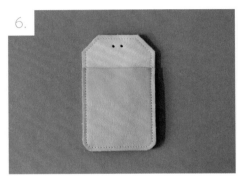

6.

1. Cut the pattern pieces from the leather. For clean round edges on the bottom of the tag, just cut the corners with right angles and leave them that way for now. Pierce the markings into the leather with an awl.

2. Tape the front piece on top of the back piece with the wrong sides together.

3. Tape the pocket piece to the front of the tag. Apply the tape only along the side and bottom edges of the pocket piece. The wrong side of the pocket piece should face the front of the tag.

4. To cut the round edges on the bottom of the tag, lay the pattern for the pocket on the taped luggage tag and carefully cut the curves using a very sharp craft knife, ideally with a fresh blade.

5. Topstitch the tag from the front. The stitch should be about 1/8 inch (3 mm) from the edge.

6. Using the pattern markings as a guide, punch the two holes at the top of the tag with a rotary punch.

7.

8.

7. With a craft knife, very carefully join the two punched holes by cutting a slit between them with a craft knife.

8. Finally, fold the string in half. Pull the folded end through the hole and make a loop.

# The Sierksdorf
## Weekender

HOLD EVERYTHING YOU WILL NEED FOR A
WEEKEND AT THE LAKE.

Several practical details make this bag your perfect
overnight companion: an outer pocket, adjustable and
removable straps, and a sturdy leather base. The contrast-
colored straps add visual interest. The sewing instructions
for this project are extensive, and a fair amount of material
is needed. For this reason, the Weekender is best for more
advanced sewers.

**LEVEL: ADVANCED**

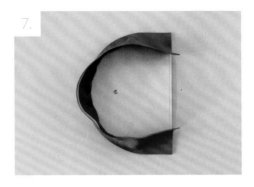

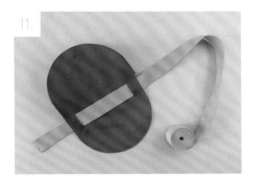

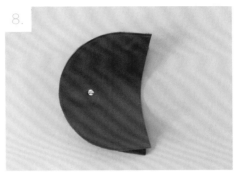

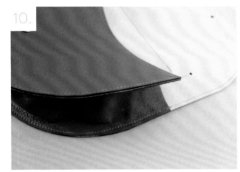

7. Apply two strips of double-sided tape along the long side of the side piece and peel off the backing. Affix the long edge of the front piece to the curved edge of the side piece. The wrong side of the leather should face the bonded leather.

8. Stitch the taped seam from the front of the leather. Keep your stitch a consistent ⅛ inch (3 mm) from the cut edge.

9. Repeat Steps 7 and 8 to stitch the back/flap piece to the side piece.

10. Apply the leather edge dressing to the curved edges of the bag. The dressing will lightly stain and seal the edges of the leather.

11. Pull the webbing through the slits at the top of the bag. Measure exactly how long you want the strap to be. The only way to adjust the strap length later is to tie a knot in the webbing.

12. Sew both open ends of the strap together, preferably with a tight zigzag stitch. Before you sew, make sure that the webbing isn't twisted. Hide the seam by sliding it under the flap.

## TIP

To give the bag a little more softness, tape a layer of fleece interfacing between the leather and bonded leather lining. Cut the fleece interfacing about ⅜ inch (1 cm) smaller than the pattern pieces.

# The Jurata
## Quilted
## Crossbody Bag

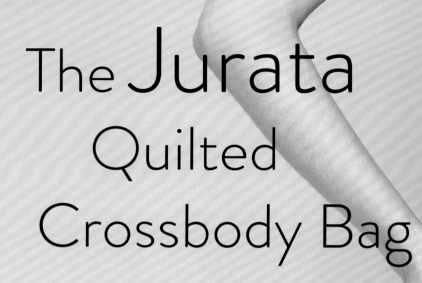

**A BAG THAT IS BIG ENOUGH FOR ALL YOUR DAILY ESSENTIALS.**

The design for this crossbody bag in faux suede is a little more elaborate than the other projects in the book. The outside of the bag is quilted with diagonal stitching and sewn with contrast-colored thread. The strap is adjustable and removable. The bag also has a zipper closure.

**LEVEL: ADVANCED**

## MATERIALS

⅓ yard (25 cm) of faux suede

2 D-rings, each ¾ inches (20 mm) in diameter

2 swivel hooks, each 1½ inches (40 mm) in diameter

1 strap slide for 1½-inch (40 mm) wide webbing

#5 closed-end zipper (for the outside of the bag), 11¾ inches (30 cm) long

#5 closed-end zipper (for the inside of the bag), 6¼ inches (16 cm) long

2 yards (180 cm) of webbing, 1½ inches (40 mm) wide

About ¼ yard (22 cm) of lining material

About ¼ yard (20 cm) of interfacing

1¾ yards (160 cm) of bias tape to finish the inside seams

About 60 inches (152 cm) of plastic cording or string for the piping

## TOOLS

Paper, pen, masking tape, and scissors for the patterns

Sewing machine, needles, and thread

Thread in a contrasting color for the quilting

Craft knife

Awl

Metal ruler

Double-sided tape

Binder clips

Pinking shears

## PATTERN PIECES (Pattern Sheet D)

### Faux Suede

2 × 2.16 AVR Jurata Quilted Crossbody Bag Front and Back

1 × 2.16 AB Jurata Quilted Crossbody Bag Base

2 × 2.16 AIO Jurata Quilted Crossbody Bag Top

2 × 2.16 SL Jurata Quilted Crossbody Bag D-ring Loop

### Lining Material

2 × 2.16 AIO Jurata Quilted Crossbody Bag Top

2 × 2.16 IVR Jurata Quilted Crossbody Bag Front and Back Lining

1 × 2.16 IB Jurata Quilted Crossbody Bag Base Lining

1 × 1.3.5 IT Inside Pocket

1 × 1.3.5 BE Inside Pocket Facing (optional)

### Fleece Interfacing

2 × 2.16 VVR Jurata Quilted Crossbody Bag Interfacing Front and Back

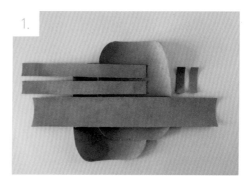

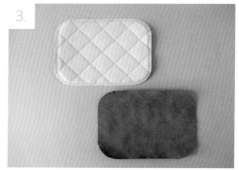

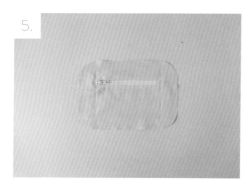

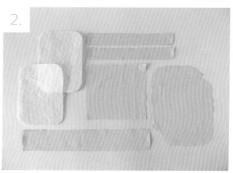

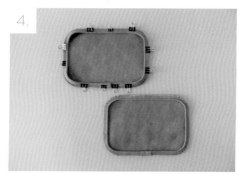

1. Carefully cut the pieces from the faux suede. Transfer all the pattern markings to the wrong side using a marking pen. Trace the diagonal markings with an awl.

2. Cut the pieces from the lining and the interfacing. Transfer the pattern markings for the inside pocket to the wrong side of the lining.

3. Tape a fleece interfacing piece to the wrong side of the front and back pieces. With the thread in the contrasting color, carefully stitch along the pattern markings to create the decorative quilted pattern on the suede. To keep the interfacing from moving, the stitches should be sewn diagonally. When you are finished with the quilting, switch out the contrast-colored thread.

4. Make two pieces of piping, each 29$^{15}$/$_{16}$ inches (76 cm) long (pages 38–39). Stitch one piece of piping to the front piece and one to the back. Position the beginning and end of each piping piece on the bottom edge of the bag. Join the ends together (page 40).

5. Make the inside zippered pocket and sew the pocket onto the right side of either the front or back lining piece (pages 29–32).

6. Tape the zipper to one of the suede top pieces, right sides together. Leave enough space between the edge of the suede and the teeth of the zipper to allow the zipper to open and close without interference. Sew the pieces together.

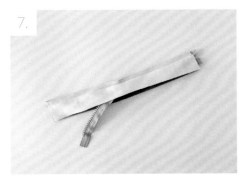

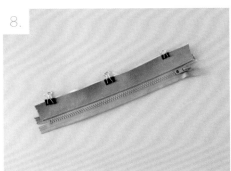

7. Tape one of the top lining pieces onto the zipper. The right side of the lining should face the wrong side of the zipper. Sew the lining along the seam between the suede and the zipper exactly. This is easiest to do if the suede is facing up and the zipper is between the suede and lining. If the zipper pull is in the way, you can open the zipper.

8. Clip or tape back the suede and lining so that the zipper is visible. Topstitch the suede with a row of stitches that is parallel to the zipper. This will make the zipper easier to open and close.

9. Repeat Steps 6–8 for the other side of the zipper and the remaining suede and top lining pieces.

10. Fold the D-ring holders into loops, lay a D-ring in each. Sew the ends closed with a 5/16-inch (8 mm) seam allowance.

11. Place a D-ring holder on each end of the zipper. Line up the seam of the D-ring holder with the edges of the zipper. Tape the holders to the zipper.

12. Place the suede base piece on top of the zipper and D-ring holders, right sides together. The end of the base should line up with the edge of the zipper.

13.

14.

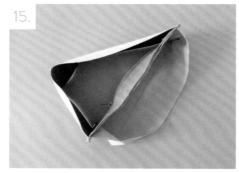

15.

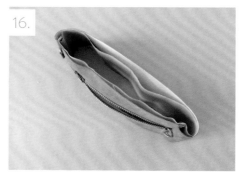

16.

17.

18.

13. Sew the pieces together. Your sewn pieces should look like what is shown in photo 13.

14. Place the base lining piece on top of the zipper, right sides together.

15. Repeat Steps 12–14 on the other side of the piece.

16. Turn the lining and the suede pieces right side out.

17. To prevent the seam allowances on the top from sticking out later, fold the ends of the base piece down and carefully topstitch them from the outside of the top piece.

18. Open the zipper (if it is not already). Clip or tape together the edges of the front piece to the edges of the side of the bag, which is made up of the combined top and base pieces. The right sides should face each other. Sew directly on top of the piping seam.

19. Repeat Step 18 for the back of the bag.

20. The bag should be inside out at this point. Lay the lining pieces for the front and back of the bag on the stitched front and back pieces, wrong sides down. The inside pocket zipper should be visible. Sew them in place. After sewing, trim away any extra lining fabric with pinking shears. Be sure to always stay within the seam allowance so that you don't sew over the piping. It can be difficult to make a tidy seam because you are sewing many layers at once. Luckily, this seam is covered with bias tape in the next step.

21. Bind the exposed seams with bias tape and then turn the bag right side out.

22. To make the adjustable shoulder strap, fold one end of the webbing around the end of a swivel hook. Sew the loose end to the strap with a tight zigzag stitch.

23. Pull the other end of the strap through the front of strap slide, the other swivel hook, and the back of the strap slide. Leave enough webbing between the end of the strap and the slide to ensure that the sewing machine foot doesn't come too close to the slide.

24. Sew the end of the webbing to the strap, as described in Step 22. To attach the strap to the bag, clip the swivel hooks to the D-rings. Adjust the strap length as needed.

## VARIATION
This bag can also be created without the contrast quilting. You can also leave out the fleece interfacing, if you don't want the extra padding.

# DESIGN VARIATIONS AND CUSTOMIZATION

When you make your own bag, it's always one-of-a-kind. Should you choose to personalize the designs in this book, the possibilities for making a project your own are endless. You can start by considering alternative materials, variations on the outside pockets, and scaling the size of your projects. Leather dye can be used to change the color of entire pieces of leather or to accentuate specific details. Embossing stamps allow you to add your initials, a special message, or your own label or logo.

## ALTERNATIVE MATERIALS

One simple way to personalize your sewing project is to use a different material than the one called for in the book. Just remember that a different material might behave differently when it's being sewn and may affect the look and feel of your finished product. For example, a bag made with an alternative fabric would have a different stiffness and drape differently. If you choose an alternative material, consider whether the seam allowances or finishes will need to be adapted. If you're using faux leather instead of real leather, all seams should be finished because the raw edges on faux leather can fray easily.

## OUTSIDE POCKET VARIATIONS

Another way to customize your leather accessories is to use a different design for the outside pockets, especially for projects like the Dänholm Backpack (page 84) or Sierksdorf Weekender (page 98). Instead of a pocket with rounded edges, you could make yours with square or trapezoidal corners.

## RESIZING AND SCALING

To change the size of a project and leave the same proportions, you can simply shrink or enlarge the pattern and adapt the seam allowances accordingly. To change the proportions, you can cut the pattern apart, make your adjustments, and put it back together again.

RESIZING AND SCALING THE REWAL DRAWSTRING BAG

## DYEING AND PAINTING LEATHER

You can change the color of leather or add embellishments using special leather dyes or paints. Because both of these substances penetrate the material, any change in color will be permanent. The dye will not flake or peel off. Leather paint usually has a very liquid consistency, so it works just as well for painting larger surface areas as it does for emphasizing small details. You can also try applying the paint using separate brush strokes. Leather dye or paint can be added to a project before or after you finish sewing.

## EMBOSSING LEATHER

You can give your leather accessories a personal touch by using embossers and stamps. Custom embossers are inexpensive and can be made of different materials, such as magnesium or brass. You will need a press to use an embosser to ensure you evenly distribute the pressure used to stamp the leather. Leather alphabet stamps or stamps with other symbols are a cheaper option and are available online and in stores. They can be punched into the leather using a mallet—a press is not needed. The downside of stamps is that it can be difficult to align the letters and decorative elements.

## LEFTOVER LEATHER

You will always have pieces of leftover leather when you're making leather accessories, but the scraps can be used in other projects. A key chain is one example. Scraps of leather from different projects can also be sewn together patchwork-style and made into bags, pillows, and poufs.

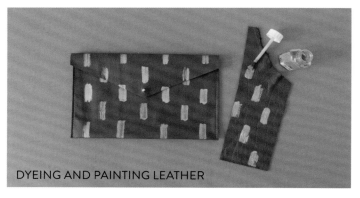

DYEING AND PAINTING LEATHER

EMBOSSED LEATHER

PROJECTS WITH LEFTOVER LEATHER

# LEATHER CARE

Once you have finished your leather handbag, you can treat the bag with a variety of products to prepare it for regular use. Products containing beeswax smell nice and leave leather feeling soft. These products can also be used to remove small spots on leather. Use a dry, soft cloth, a sock, or a fine sponge to massage the product into the leather evenly. Leave the product on the leather for a while and then polish it once more. The color of the leather may darken when you apply the product, but the leather usually returns to its original color.

You can also waterproof leather by applying a spray-on waterproofing finish evenly onto the leather. Use the spray according to the manufacturer's instructions, ideally outdoors. Waterproofing can cause the leather to darken slightly.

Leather cannot be washed. If washed, it hardens, shrinks, and can become brittle. Special leather cleaners are available in stores. You can use these if there are stains on bags or accessories (although it won't be possible to remove all types of stains). In addition to these options, some dry cleaners also offer leather cleaning and leather care services.

Leather can sometimes discolor lighter fabrics, but these discolorations will usually come out in the wash.

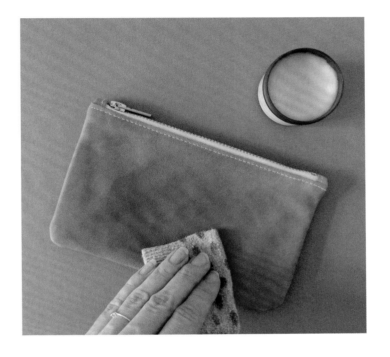

# TROUBLESHOOTING COMMON PROBLEMS

## IF THE LEATHER IS TOO THICK TO BEGIN SEWING

On home sewing machines, it's common for the foot to have difficulty moving over the leather if it's too thick. If this happens, it can help to use a presser foot spacer, ideally one that attaches to the machine, or a leather one that you make yourself (page 44). At the start of a seam, the spacer is placed behind the material; it raises the back of the foot so it is parallel to the throat plate and allows the material to be fed through more easily.

## IF THE CORNERS ARE TOO THICK

Sometimes, sewing can become difficult when several layers of leather meet at the seams. You can try to sew very carefully and slowly, or advance the hand wheel manually. This way, you can feel whether it's really possible to sew through the layers and minimize the risk of breaking your needle. If the leather is just too thick, there is unfortunately no other option than to sew it by hand. When sewing by hand, try to keep the stitch length consistent. The holes can be pre-punched using an awl or specialized leather hole punches, if necessary.

## IF YOU SEW SOMETHING INCORRECTLY

For minor errors, it's sometimes enough to just separate the seam carefully and sew it again. Make sure that the old needle holes are in the seam allowance and won't be visible on the finished bag. For major sewing errors, the only real solution is to cut another piece of leather and start over.

## IF THE NEEDLE DOESN'T SEW THROUGH THE LEATHER CORRECTLY OR YOU NOTICE SKIPPED STITCHES

Sometimes, the needle won't go through the leather correctly or the machine starts skipping stitches when you sew with double-sided tape. To keep the adhesive from gumming up the needle, it's a good idea to wipe it off with your fingers in between seams. For heavier buildup, wet a cotton ball with nail polish remover and wipe off the needle. This should clean the needle, and it should have no trouble sewing through the leather.

## IF YOUR THREAD UNRAVELS

There could be several different reasons for your thread to unravel. When you're sewing through thicker areas, some threads might not be smooth enough to be fed through the needle correctly. Another possibility is that the needle hole is a little too narrow and the thread can't pass through the eye properly. A third possibility is that the needle is not positioned correctly in the sewing machine. If the needle is bent, it cannot enter into the fabric properly. Often, it's enough to replace the needle with a new, slightly larger needle. If you're sewing with double-sided tape, it's also important to wipe the adhesive off the needle periodically or remove it with nail polish remover.

# GLOSSARY

## AWL
An awl is an essential leatherworking tool that is used to transfer a specific marking from a pattern to a piece of leather, or to carefully mark where a seam will be placed.

## BIAS TAPE
Bias tape can be used to neatly bind edges and protect the edges of your materials from fraying. Premade bias tape is available in a variety of colors and widths. If you want your bias tape to come from a specific fabric, it is easy to make your own. You cut a strip of fabric on the bias, or diagonally (at a 45° angle) across the grain. The strip should be four times as wide as you want the finished bias tape to be. Fold the fabric strip in half lengthwise and iron. Unfold the fabric again, then fold the left and right sides to the center crease and press firmly. The sides will form the seam allowances, and the center crease will lay on top of the edge that you are finishing. If your strip of bias tape is not long enough for your project, you can sew several individual strips together, as described on page 42.

## BINDER CLIPS
Binder clips are used in place of pins when sewing with leather to avoid poking holes through the material.

## BINDING
This term refers to the finishing or reinforcing of seams and edges. Bias tape, elastic binding tape, and (if your sewing machine can handle it) leather strips work well for binding. For more information on using bias tape, see page 38.

## DOUBLE-SIDED TAPE
Double-sided tape is used in leatherworking, alongside binder clips, to temporarily hold individual pieces together until they are sewn. Double-sided tape is especially handy for attaching zippers because it is flat and clear (page 30). It does not need to be removed after sewing.

## DRAWSTRING CASING
A drawstring casing on a bag or pouch is a tube of fabric through which a cord can be drawn. It is sewn with two parallel seams.

## PATTERN PIECE
A pattern is made up of various pattern pieces. The pattern pieces are cut from the selected material and, when sewn together, make up the finished accessory.

## PIPING
Piping is a type of trim and embellishment that accentuates seams and stabilizes a design. It is common for piping to be made of leather. For information on making piping, see pages 38–41.

## PRESSER FEET
Various types of presser feet are used to make it easier to sew leather, zippers, and piping. Even topstitching close to the material edge is made easier with a special foot. The presser feet you buy should be made for your particular sewing machine.

## RIGHT SIDE
The right side of a piece of fabric or leather is the "pretty" side. For leather, this is the skin, finished, or embossed side, or the side with the nicer nap. For fabric, it is the printed side or the side with the clearer weave pattern. It faces outward on the finished accessory. The right sides of your material often face each other when you're sewing. Later on, when the project is turned right side out, the seam allowances will be on the inside and the nice side of the material will be on the outside.

## SEAM ALLOWANCE
The term refers to the distance between the seam and the cut edge of the material. The desired seam allowance varies depending on the type of fabric and seam finishing. For leather, a typical seam allowance is ¼–⅜ inch

(8–10 mm). For fabric, it may be as wide as ½ inch (1.5 cm). All the projects in this book use a ⅜-inch (1 cm) seam allowance unless noted otherwise in the instructions. Markings from a pattern are always transferred to the seam allowance of the cut pattern piece. The most commonly used seam allowances are marked on the throat plate of the sewing machine. If your desired seam allowance is not listed, you can mark it yourself with a piece of tape. This method is makes the seam allowances easy to see, and the tape is easy to remove later on. Be sure to carefully line up the edge of your material along the piece of tape.

## SEAM FINISHING, FINISHING

There are different ways to finish seams depending on the type of material used. The purpose of seam finishing is to keep a seam from unraveling and to give it a polished look. Leather does not fray or usually require any finishing if a lining is used. Even lining often doesn't require any finishing because the seam allowance is hidden. For handbags without a lining, however, all visible inside seams should be finished. This can be achieved by using bias tape or, for very thin materials, a zigzag stitch right along the edge.

## THREAD TENSION

The upper thread tension on a sewing machine can be adjusted to create balanced-looking stitches. The top side of the seam usually looks better than the bottom, so always sew with that in mind.

## TOPSTITCHING

A topstitch is a line of stitches that remains visible after you've finished your project. This type of stitch is often sewn in a straight line parallel to an edge. For leather and accessories, topstitching is usually sewn about ⅛ inch (3 mm) from the edge of your material.

## WRONG SIDE

The wrong side of a piece of fabric or leather is the less "pretty" side. It faces the inside of the finished accessory, so it is less visible. The wrong side often faces up or out while you work. Markings are also made on the wrong side of a piece of fabric or leather, which allows the right side to remain untouched.

# RESOURCES

Shopping for leather in person at a local shop is highly recommended. You will get a feel of what the leather feels (and smells) like. You can also bring a pattern and make sure it fits on your desired hide. If you do choose to shop online, here are some additional resources.

For leather:
- **Tandy Leather**, tandyleather.com
- **Ohio Travel Bag**, ohiotravelbag.com
- **Ecopell**, vegetable-tanned-leather.com

For leatherworking tools and hardware:
- **Tandy Leather**, tandyleather.com
- **Prym**, prym-consumer-usa.com

For thread:
- **Gütermann**, guetermann.com/en

For fabric and interfacing:
- **Mood Fabrics**, moodfabrics.com

# INDEX

## ABOUT THE AUTHOR

Kasia Ehrhardt lives and works with her partner, daughter, and cat in Berlin. She creates patterns and sewing instructions for backpacks, handbags, and accessories for the DIY Sewing Academy. She studied architecture at Columbia University in New York and then worked as an architect. Along the way, she also took courses in accessories design at the Fashion Institute of Technology. There, she learned to design and produce handbags, shoes, belts, and other accessories, mainly using leather. She also learned how to make technical drawings and patterns and write instructions. Kasia returned to Germany in 2009 and turned her focus to developing a collection, creating patterns, and making prototypes and samples for accessories. She also makes custom leather bags for her label KSIA. By doing this work, Kasia is reviving a family tradition—her great-grandfather made leather suitcases and bags over a hundred years ago. Kasia enjoys working with leather because it is such a durable material that is also soft and supple.

## FIND KASIA ONLINE

Website and blog: ksia-berlin.de

DIY Sewing Academy: diysa.wordpress.com

Pinterest: pinterest.com/KSIA

Find patterns, sewing instructions, and material at DaWanda: de.dawanda.com/shop/DIY-Sewing-Academy

Patterns and sewing instructions on Etsy: etsy.com/shop/DIYSewingAcademy

Kasia has also created a course in making leather handbags for makerist.de, the online school for makers: makerist.de/courses/category/naehen_lernen

# ACKNOWLEDGMENTS

A huge thank you to my boyfriend Eric Steinfurth for his love and support. My family Sophia, Grazyna, and Winfried Ehrhardt deserve a big thank you for their moral support and for putting up with me when I had my head buried in a project. Many thanks to my school friend Gesa Kunter for the technical advice for this book, to Sabrina Weigt for the fabulous photo styling, and to photographer Sebastian Donath for his expertise, organization, and patience. Thanks also to the wonderful models and Jazmin Lois Rodriquez for hair and make-up. Thank you to Linda Jamnongware and Gerald Schmidt for photography and image processing tips and tricks, Amy Campos for the transatlantic photo fun, and my friends Berit Müller, Sandra Kloska, Silke Wolter, and Gesa Lüthje—I'm always in good company with you. And thanks to my traveling and cooking buddy Kwi-Hae Kim and to Johanna Krüger and family. A million thanks to my creative companions Maja Fodermeyer, Christine Hornicke, and Katja Muñoz for your support and ideas. Thanks to the team at Makerist.de, especially Amber Riedl, who developed the idea into a video tutorial on sewing leather. Last but not least, thank you to my daughter Theodora, who came into the world while this book was being made.

Finally, thank you also to the following companies, without whom many of the prototypes, samples, and designs in this book would not have been possible: Stoffe.de (fabfab GmbH) for fabric, wool felt, leather, faux leather, Alcantara, and accessories, such as cording, webbing, and bias tape; Ecopell GmbH for the naturally tanned leather; Prym for the tools and accessories; Swafing for the sturdy canvas material, and Gütermann for the thread.

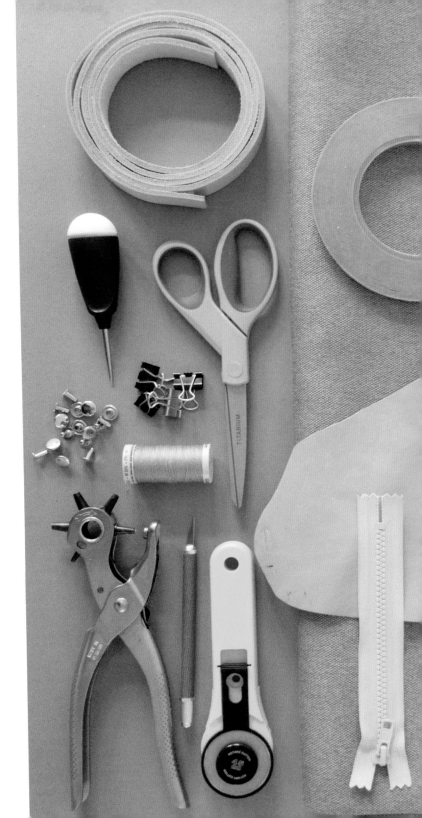